THE ULTIMATE
ISLAND

AMIT OFFIR

The Ultimate Island

Amit Offir

Contact: amitoffir@gmail.com

Official website: www.amitoffir.com

Translation from the Hebrew: Nava Namdar

ISBN 9781729065068

AMIT OFFIR

THE ULTIMATE
ISLAND

MALTA IN THE GRASP
of YOUR HAND

Contents

ABOUT THE AUTHOR

Amit Offir is the best-selling author of many books, a world traveler, an adventurer and a sought-after lecturer. Among his books are: "Travel the World and Make Money," "24/8 – The Secret of Being Mega-Effective," "Consciousness of Abundance" "Whispers," as well as many inspirational travel books, drawing books and empowerment books on various subjects.

Amit's passion for traveling motivates him, year after year, to travel to the most exotic places in the world, so he can personally experience the special attractions offered to travelers. During his trips he explores the place by seeking the magic surrounding it and then shares his insights and experiences with his readers. This unique way of traveling not only enables him to experience the journey at higher levels and make the most out of it, but also transforms the trip into a tool for personal and business development and even helps increasing his income, and so it, hopefully, help you, the readers.

Amit develops and creates contents as well as techniques in various fields to help people around the world improve their quality of life and travel more frequently. He began his career as a drawing teacher and published a series of tutorial books which show, among other things, how anyone can draw any character he pleases by using only five simple steps. This original method and other methods that appear in his tutorials help children and adults of all ages all over the world enjoy their travels by learning how to draw the animals, plants, music instruments or traditional clothes that are unique to the place they travel to. His books reached the top spots in many categories on Amazon's bestseller lists on four continents, as well as in Walmart. In addition, he invented and developed the Domino Reaction Method for Time Management, the Spiral Method for personal and business growth, different sale tactics and many other processes that he teaches through his books. Amit's vision is to help as many people as possible realize their dreams.

SEARCH FOR THE ULTIMATE ISLAND

"Never interrupt your enemy when he is making a mistake."

- Napoleon Bonaparte

Every year I travel to exotic destinations and explore countries I have not yet visited, and 2018 was no different. After spending the previous year traveling to destinations like Mount Everest in Nepal, Mozambique, Vietnam, South Africa and Zanzibar, I decided this year to focus my travel in Europe.

My first trip was to Serbia where I traveled its cool and rugged mountain range area. Towards the end of my trip there, I decided to look for a sunnier and warmer location to go to next. I asked myself what was important to me and I wrote down a few conditions I desired my next destination to include: exotic beaches, special diving sites, interesting attractions, unique culture, excellent food, and to top it off, I wanted to enjoy a vibrant nightlife.

During my time in Serbia, I realized that it was a very big country and I had to travel long hours in order to get from one place to another; therefore, for my next destination I decided to look for a smaller country where locations are closer to each other and easier to get to, so I was able to experience more in less time. A colorful ad on Facebook caught my attention: the annual MTV Festival in Malta was about to begin and that was exactly what I needed. I had just sold one of the houses I owned in the U.S. and made a nice profit. I felt proud of the work I had done and wanted to party.

In ancient times, it seemed very difficult to locate the island of Malta. In May 1565 the Sultan of the Ottoman Empire, Suleiman the Magnificent, sent a force of 40,000 Turkish troops to invade Malta, defeat and conquer the 700 Knights of Malta and a few thousand more fighters.

Against all odds, and mostly due to the inefficient functioning of the Turkish army leadership, its forces were defeated and the Turkish army, which suffered great loss, began to retreat to their ships and sail back to Constantinople. According to stories, the source of the familiar expression "Malta Yok" was first written in a report submitted by the Turkish commander of the ground forces, Mustafa Pasha, to the Sultan. Concerned for his fate, he reported that his forces simply did not locate the island of Malta, and wrote "Malta Yok," meaning Malta does not exist. The glaring problem with this kind of untruth was hiding the deaths of 8,000 soldiers who never made it back home to Turkey. The Ottoman commander was inevitably exposed upon the return of the Turkish forces and was immediately dismissed.

Today it is a bit easier to locate Malta!

Despite its miniscule size, it has drawn attention from all over the world, and has indeed much to be proud of.

The Republic of Malta is a small island country made up of several islands (only three of them are inhabited) and located in the center of the Mediterranean Sea, south of Italy. I heard you can see the lights of romantic Sicily if you look at the horizon at night from Ta'Dmejrek, the highest point in Malta located on the Dingli Cliffs. Malta itself is the main island and the largest of the three, where the majority of the population lives and where its capital Valletta is located.

The second largest island is Gozo and its capital is Victoria. Gozo is known as a quiet place, a destination designed for relaxation and rest, as well as enjoying the bars and restaurants in Victoria. In fact, many Maltese own vacation homes in Gozo where they go whenever they feel like they need to escape the hustle and bustle of the main Island of Malta.

The third largest island Comino is significantly smaller than the others, lacks paved roads, and has one lone hotel. There are only about three people living on this island on a regular basis.

Malta seems like a 'living museum' with much history and

stories of ancient crusades and battles. The strategic location of the islands in the Mediterranean Sea brought about many invasions and they were conquered again and again. The land chronicles some 7,000 years of vibrant history and filled with remnants of the past. Malta achieved independence in 1964, and became a member of the European Union in 2004.

My love for islands always immerses me in great enthusiasm and makes me feel as if I were a daring explorer from ancient times who first discovers the wonders of creation and the beauty of the world. I was also impressed by the fact that there were interesting diving sites surrounding Malta, including dozens of shipwrecks of various sizes that have provided marine life with habitats.

Malta's location and the depth of the sea around it, causes the water to be crystal clear almost all year round and the excellent visibility will allow you to see clearly up to 40 meters deep. In addition, if you are a diving enthusiast and enjoy extreme sports, you can experience the fascinating underwater scenery and go diving in caves and alcoves, where many marine creatures reside.

The decision was made.

Malta, I am on my way!

ARRIVAL IN MALTA

"Impossible is a word to be found only in the dictionary of fools."

- Napoleon Bonaparte

Malta seems to be a perfect destination in every way. I like to pack for sunny destinations and for vacations where the element of going to beaches takes up a large part of the time spent there. I packed a light suitcase in addition to a small backpack, scuba diving mask, GoPro, a professional camera, running clothes, a swimsuit and some evening clothes as well as a good book for inspiration. This time I decided to take the book "How Come That Idiot's Rich and I'm Not?" by Robert Shemin that focuses on the real estate business.

I arrived at Malta directly from Serbia using Air Malta, the flag carrier airline of Malta. The short flight (an hour and a half) passed by quickly, while I had a lively conversation with a famous Israeli director and film producer named Gil Lupo. It was his second visit to Malta, and he told me about the places he loved most on the island, and the countless movies and TV series that were filmed in Malta.

The pilot announced that we were beginning our descent into Malta. From the window, I could see the reefs and the hypnotic blue colors of the clear Mediterranean waters.

As we are about to land in Malta, I want to share with you that this book is not like any other travel book, but rather it is a reflection of the attitudes and ways of thinking I have adopted over the years, which helped me travel around the world and fulfill countless dreams. It is my hope that this book will encourage you to travel the world more often in general, and more specifically, encourage you to visit this magical country and experience it in a more powerful way which I will expand on later in this book. I wish you an enjoyable reading that will make your trip to Malta an unforgettable vacation.

Throughout my life, I have always been interested in learning new things. In contrast to the traditional approach that one should focus on one area only and not "scatter" his energy, I always felt the urge to learn about as many areas of interests as possible and to experience as many adventures as I can, even though everyone around me urged me to finish what I started.

From an early age, I learned different languages, traveled to distant places, took many courses and attended as many lectures as possible, read about subjects that interested me and allowed myself to rediscover who I was again and again. All of these helped me become an interesting person with well-developed social skills and also allowed me to build a special way of life which did not force me to give up doing the things I love, as I watched it happen to most of my friends and people that I knew. As I grew older I realized that this was the key to my happiness and I was willing to pay any price I needed to pay in order to keep the fiery passion for traveling and learning burning within me.

I remember that as a child, I already understood that there were two types of people in life: those who dream of living and those who fully live. It was clear to me that I wanted to live an exciting life and fulfill all of my dreams. When I spoke with people about my fear of living a normal life, I realized that for them it was a natural and logical way to live. For example, many people I spoke with were willing to work at a job they did not like, do things that did not interest them, and they often compromised on fulfilling their own hopes and dreams by pleasing others or because they were too afraid to try something new and fail at it. Their fear of a possible failure was stronger than their fear of the foretold defeat of their decision not to try at all.

Over the years, I have noticed that the way people think is the most important factor that determines what is possible in their lives, and what is impossible. I believe that as we get older we feel that we understand the rules of the game of life. The problem is that the more we believe in these rules, the more these rules and beliefs become a reality for us and confirms the idea that it is indeed real.

In this way, a person might believe, for example, that being a salaried employee who gets a regular paycheck is a safe and stable way to live, while another person believes that working as an employee is risky, since their fate is depended on other people's decisions, who might not have their best interest at heart. According to their beliefs, the former would prefer to be an employee, while the latter would choose to be a business owner.

The point is that to a certain extent both are right. Concurring with their perception and beliefs, life will provide them with various examples over and over again that will be seen as "proofs" of their views about life which will then enable them to continue living according to their beliefs. This way, we feel that we have some control over our lives, and that we have figured out the rules of this 'game of life'.

For many years, the desire to learn new things in different fields made me feel as if I was wasting precious energy, time and money on different areas that had no logical connection between them. The sense of frustration that I never finished anything I had started and therefore made me an irresponsible person was always in the back of my mind and made me feel that I might never find my place in the world. On the other hand, each time I found an interest in something new I could not ignore nor resist the great passion I felt towards it, which swept my whole being into a new adventure.

At the age of 25, I decided to end my studies of animation

and even though I had plenty of knowledge in many different areas, I still had no idea how they could connect to each other, and how all this knowledge I had acquired could assist my progress in life. I had practical experience in managing a hostel. I knew how to sail yachts, play the guitar and drums, surf, write books, and I even had a short experience at managing a publishing house. I also experimented with graphic design, business management, marketing, branding, sales and more, but all of these looked like unrelated threads that I could never connect and use properly.

It was many years later that all I had studied and experienced started connecting to each other and created a flame that could not be extinguished. Within this process also came the understanding that whatever I learned I could benefit from it in my life. This understanding completely changed my way of life and enabled me to live and fulfill my dreams in every field without the fears of survival and how to generate regular income.

I understood that new knowledge and experiences in life are incredibly valuable and it became a powerful force in my approach to life. That is why I started a tradition in 2014 that I keep to this day, where I choose the learning and skills I want to acquire during the following year and I always pick a challenge that seems to be unattainable or beyond the limits of my understanding. In this way, I commit myself to find creative solutions to achieve my goals, even if these goals are only partially realized. This yearly "tradition" has repeatedly made my life richer, filled it with action and accomplishments and is one of the most important decisions you can make for yourselves, if you choose to.

In 2014, for example, I decided to learn how to light a fire in the wild. The ability to make a fire in the wilderness is one of the most important survival skills, one that helped pre-historic men dominate the animal world and to be positioned at the top of the food chain. Although we no longer have to know how to light a fire, the knowledge of doing so seemed more relevant than ever.

The learning of how to make fire can be compared to daily life and the challenges of those of us who want to create stability in their lives, in business, in relationships or in their workplace. In addition, one of the important insights I have realized in my life is that you can take a skill or understanding from one field and apply it to a completely different area. In this way, it is possible to distinguish yourself from other people involved in your field and create uniqueness and advantages in the face of competition.

The first step of making a fire was the research. I watched many 'how-to' videos that taught step by step on how to create fire using different techniques. Most of the videos were short and showed that within a few minutes the target was achieved and the fire was lit. In reality, however, I discovered that there was a huge chasm between real-life and what was shown online.

The simplicity of the task as shown in the videos was light years away from the reality I experienced. The climate and the weather were different, the vegetation and the types of trees that grew in my country differed from those presented in the videos. The raw materials that people found in the explanatory videos were completely unlike those I found in my surroundings. The gap that I saw was so great that I realized that if I was to rely on the knowledge from the survival videos there was no chance I would survive in the wild in a real situation and I would probably find my death.

Week after week I went hiking and practiced lighting a fire by using only natural means and failed every time. I was also very close to succeeding many times, but something in the 'system' I created did not work for some reason. The materials I chose to build my set with were not from the same trees I saw in the instructional videos. I was unable to stabilize the system or have not found all the necessary materials. Most of the time I simply was not experienced enough to find the softwood and had to work with hardwood, which was much harder to light up and required experience and skill that I had not yet possessed. For four months I walked around with a sense of frustration. The theoretical studies were not enough. At some point I hired a survival specialist and spent a day out in the field with him. Though he gave me plenty of advice, modified and corrected the process together with me, we still could not achieve the goal of lighting a fire in the wild. It was as if the universe was trying to make it difficult for me in order to test my determination.

Despite the obstacles and the desire to give up on this goal, I decided to stick to the task no matter how long it took me. Despite my frustration, I knew that with every attempt I was getting closer to the sweet moment of success. I continued to fail time after time until finally, after four months and ten days I succeeded!

When the fiery flames finally lit up and danced in front of me, the feeling I felt must have been similar to that of the ancient man seeing fire for the first time ever! I could not contain the exhilaration and happiness of my new accomplishment as I shouted in the thick of the forest: 'FIRRRRRE!!'

That moment of success was so worth the hard work I put into it and I consider it a defining moment, as I felt how I regain control over my life. I felt invulnerable and I knew I could manage anywhere I found myself at.

Two years later, in 2016, I traveled to an African village in Mozambique and lived there for three months. This time I packed another unusual challenge I was interested in conquering - I decided to learn how to climb the coconut tree. I was greatly attracted to this challenge because I believed that in extreme situations it could save my life.

During my visit to Sri Lanka several years ago, I heard many stories about people who survived the tsunami that hit the island in 2004, thanks to their ability to climb the coconut trees that grew in that area. Those stories sparked my imagination and inspired me to learn how to climb these trees, even if it was for the mere purpose of picking a fresh coconut and drinking its sweet juices on a hot summer day. As with the fire video tutorials, watching the locals do it made it look so easy, as though they were not making any effort. I believed that within a few minutes I would also succeed.

My first climb attempt made it clear to me that it was not as simple as it looked and that in order to succeed I would have to practice gradually and carefully. I was often injured during my attempts and realized how difficult this life skill could be for unskilled people. It took me two months to finally succeed in the mission, and my perseverance paid off and taught me a lot about determination.

As I continued to explore my limits in regards to the rules of 'the game of my life' I found more and more ways to fulfill my dreams and fewer reasons why not to do so. Continuously, over the years, I felt that I was developing a 'muscle' that is setting me free!

I believe people need to strive to fulfill their dreams because the world would be a better place if people were happier. Today, I know that everything is possible. When we aim high and keep on our path we can achieve incredible feats. I choose to live in a world where the rules of the game say that everything is allowed and within my reach as long as I honor and respect others and never hurt another being.

I hope that reading this book will inspire you to flex the rules of the game of your life and that when you are done reading you will be open to more possibilities in your life and to subsequently re-adjust your life track.

Do not hesitate to contact me with any questions you may have. My contact information appears at the beginning of this book.

Enjoy!

THE DECISION TO TRAVEL MORE OFTEN

"Death is nothing, but to live defeated and inglorious is to die daily."

- Napoleon Bonaparte

Over the years, many people have asked me to help them create a lifestyle that will allow them to travel more often and live their lives with more passion and joy. They tell me that when they look at my photographs from my travels around the world, they are filled with inspiration that causes them to stop the race of life and ask themselves what their dreams are and how they can be realized before it is too late.

I noticed that my learning curve was significantly higher during my travels than at other times and over time I began connecting the trips I had taken with the success and improvements that occurred in my life. The more I traveled the freer I became, disentangling myself from the formula of being enslaved to the office and the regular job. With every trip I took, more business opportunities were presented to me and allowed me to continue traveling without any financial worries.

Ever since my first major trip to South America in 2000 and to this day I have been trying to travel for at least a few months a year and use the trips as a tool for personal and business development. In 2016 I began integrating my clients into various 'empowerment journeys' that I organized, during which they received professional business training combined with life coaching, and so together we were moving towards building them the wonderful lifestyle so many people aspire to.

If you take a moment to think about it, it makes perfect sense; when we travel we break away from our busy schedule and open up to new ideas. I noticed that during a vacation I become super creative and so I am able to inspect my life and my business from a different perspective, find different solutions or experience a breakthrough. Oftentimes, my most brilliant ideas came to me during a trip which then helped my business grow significantly. Just like a muscle grows while it is resting, we grow while we are on a break from our hectic everyday routine. We need to take trips to inspire us and awaken the passion for life resides in us.

During my travels around the world, I learned many things I could not learn anywhere else. I learned new languages, social skills, navigations, and how to cope with the many different situations I found myself in. I learned from books that I finally had time to read, I met many people who changed my life, I learned to dance, cook, surf and love. I learned about money, responsibility, commitment, self-defense and many ways to survive in nature. I learned about business and the ache of longing. I learned much about what I love and what I want to do with my life. I learned to love myself and had countless opportunities to test my abilities and limitations. I learned about managing my fears and to overcome them. I learned to try new things, to make mistakes and to forgive myself.

I see people that travel to great destinations but complain constantly, others who argue and disagree with each other. Some who spend a lot of money on a trip but find ways to see only the negative, and there are those who stay in their hotel pool throughout the trip because it is an all-inclusive vacation and do not want to pay for anything else.

There are many factors that can turn our vacation into a complete failure. Some of them could be choosing an unsuitable trip partner, joining an organized tour that is not well managed, traveling to an exotic destination that turns out to be disappointing, poor decision-making or inability to make decisions, limiting beliefs, a critical and judgmental mind, as well as many other reasons.

In addition, going on a trip often takes us out of our comfort zone, where we have to deal with many things we are not used to. As I traveled more frequently, I found additional ways to make my vacations and trips more and more profitable and worthwhile. During some vacations, I have written books that have been sold around the world for many years. During other trips I have taken, I met influential people who helped me expand my business. I learned many things that helped my professional development in my fields of expertise.

The photographs I had taken were published in various magazines, I was interviewed by the media as an expert in my field in the countries I visited, I have often held coaching sessions or work meetings in exotic places for tourists or locals and, of course, the vacation and rest themselves provide such great inspiration and were the greatest source for terrific ideas, which were eventually applied and turned into businesses, entrepreneurial ventures and different projects for me.

Today, this way of thinking allows me to travel as much as I want, without concern for the cost of a vacation, and without the fear of missing workdays, and losing income. In my book "Travel the World and Make Money" I have expanded on the various ways of saving money on trips, as well as providing knowledge on how you can make money while traveling. In this book, I will expand a little on the various approaches that may turn a simple recreational travel into an empowering journey, and a life-altering experience. Throughout the book, I will include experiences from my trip to Malta that you can experience yourself, once you go on your own vacation to the island.

It is funny to think about it this way but we had never been taught how to have fun on a trip, and most of us do not really know how to be happy or fulfill our dreams. The truth is that it is logical and natural that we do not know as every skill in life one has to practice and specialize in. Traveling well is a matter of skill and when I realized it, I felt a strong need to explore the area of effective vacations so that I could continuously take trips all over the world. In order to succeed in fulfilling this dream, I began to formulate guidelines and principles that will help me maximize and utilize trips I took for the purpose of my personal professional and business development. This allows me to travel without compromising or giving up on a vacation because of the cost.

Today I know that taking vacations and going on trips are profitable assets and excellent investments. They are more than just an expense and therefore I do not hesitate when it is time to make a decision about taking my next vacation. I will expand further on the things you can do to make your trip a powerful, meaningful and unforgettable experience.

DAY 1

Valletta - The Diminutive City of Knights

"Do not wait... the time to act will never be perfect."

- Napoleon Bonaparte

The advantage of Malta's 'size' worked in my favor from the moment I landed. Upon my arrival, I took a taxi to the Seashells Resort at Suncrest, where I was staying during my vacation. The location of the hotel was excellent and enabled me to quickly get to anywhere I wanted to go to on the island. The hotel room was spacious, indulging, and had a balcony overlooking the sea.

To get into vacation mode quickly, I took a quick shower and changed into fresh clothes. My experience taught me it could take some time to ease into the vacation mode, maybe hours or even days, as we continue to act as if we are still at work and under stress. We might take our busy daily routine into our vacation and the fear that our customers will leave us because we took a trip. We might overuse our cell phone or addictively surf the internet, as well as our social networks or news sites. This makes it difficult for us to relax into our vacation and to feel truly free. It can take our bodies some time to get used to the idea that we are away on a vacation. In the meantime the vacation is passing by quickly, as we miss out on activities and sites to see.

The 'quickness' factor is an essential matter. Our brain takes time to synchronize with reality. It takes us about 15 minutes to feel full after we eat, for example, even though in reality the food is already in our body. Some people need several days to 'leave the office' even though they had already begun their vacation, boarded a plane or reached an exotic destination on the other side of the world. In their minds, they are still at the office, worrying about their clients or preoccupied with other things that trouble them. By the time they are set into the 'vacation mode', they find that it is already over and they need to get back home, to their daily routines.

It takes time to get into vacation mode and let go of all the thoughts, tensions and the everyday burden. The time it takes us to lose all of those depends on our skill.

When I realized this, I began exploring the things that helped me get into my vacation faster and over the years I improved my ability to shift from one experience to another in a minimum amount of time. I prioritize my travel over anything else, so I can maximize the vacation experience and avoid wasting valuable time.

First I slip into comfortable shoes and clothes that I enjoy wearing. Second, I make sure I pack as little gear as possible. Taking small and light suitcases makes the whole trip experience simpler and more enjoyable. I like to have my favorite music playing in my ears and a good book to read during the trip, preferably one that discusses distant locations that ignite my imagination. I also recommend taking a shower right when you arrive in your destination, it might help you adjust quicker. If a shower is not going to refresh you, try to find something that works for you like getting a massage or having a glass of wine to toast the launching of your vacation, maybe changing into more comfortable clothes, or walking around the hotel; anything that makes you feel fresher and allows you to enjoy all the beauty and richness the world has to offer you at your location.

The first item on my trip agenda was to visit the capital city of Malta, Valletta. Valletta is considered the smallest capital city in the European Union, at only about half a square kilometer, and one of the world's smallest capital cities. The official name of the city was given to it by the Knights of Malta who used to entitle it as Humilissima Civitas, which means "the most modest city." With the expansion and growth of the city it was given the opposite adjective of Superbissima, which translates into "the proudest." Nowadays, residents of the city call it Il-Belt which means "The City" in Maltese.

The taxi driver dropped me off at the entrance to the city and at first glance I felt that I had gone back in time to the

Middle Ages. Enormous historic buildings, monuments, and lively streets welcomed me as if the city had come to life in my honor. A distant ringing of bells greeted me and as I entered the old alleyways, I felt as if I was engulfed in the thousands of years of countless stories that had built this city.

One of the stories that drew my attention was the story of the establishment of the city of Valletta, following the Great Siege of Malta. In 1522, the Roman Emperor, Charles V, granted control over Malta to the Knights of Malta in order to restrain the conquests of Sultan Suleiman the Magnificent, who was busy establishing his empire and had already conquered the Greek island of Rhodes. After the knights began attacking the Turkish ships, and even endangered their shipping routes, the Ottoman Empire decided to invade the island and to end the Knights' rule of Malta. The Great Siege on Malta began in 1565. A huge force of about 30,000 Turkish soldiers landed on the island of Malta, and a month later another 10,000 Turkish troops arrived.

Against this Ottoman force stood the Order of the Knights, led by Jean de la Valette and counted about 600 to 700 knights with a few thousand soldiers under them. The Turks enforced a long siege on the island; however, time after time the Knights resisted and pushed off the invading forces, causing heavy losses on the Ottoman army. After almost four months, the Turkish forces were forced to evacuate the remnants of their forces from the island, following the arrival of strong Christian reinforcements to help the besieged Knights. The end of the siege brought about the foundation of Malta in 1566, by the head of the Order, Jean de la Valette.

The days of fighting in Malta did not end there. In 1798, Malta was conquered by Napoleon, and two years later was occupied again, this time by the British who ruled it for a very long time. World War II did not skip over Malta either. During the war, the city suffered great losses due to German and Italian bombings during the siege of the island.

The story of Malta has a happy ending since on September 21st, 1964, it gained its independence and Valletta became the capital of the country.

Valletta fascinated me despite its small size and I spent many hours visiting its many great and interesting historical sites. The fact that it lies on the Sciberras peninsula and surrounded by sea on three of its sides, gives it a special and surprising structure. To its north is the port of Marsamxett, to its south the big port, and to its east the Mediterranean Sea. In the west, Valletta is bordered by the city of Floriana.

It is worth knowing that the city is formed in a crisscrossed pattern of seven streets in length, and eight blocks in width, so that it is very easy to navigate, and is easy to find your way to all its important sites, including the Barrakka Gardens, which were established as a private garden of the

Knights of Malta in 1661 and opened to the public in 1824. I visited the gardens twice during my visit to Malta, one time during daytime and the other in moonlight. A short visit to the gardens will have you enjoy the romantic atmosphere, stunning scenery and impressive historical relics, including tablets and panels that tell the story of Malta; past and present events, statues of famous figures, and sculptures from the island.

Malta is kind of a wonderful time machine. It is perhaps one of the few places in the world where you can behold 7,000 years of history that are displayed side by side as if it were its natural state.

If you are a fan of culture and history you definitely reached paradise. Valletta is filled with rare historical works of art. In the fourth chapel, for example, you will find a painting depicting the beheading of John the Baptist by the Italian artist Caravaggio. Another painting depicts St. Jerome, who was one of the fathers of the Catholic Church.

At the corner of merchant's street (Triq il-Merkanti) you will find the 18th-century municipality building of Valletta, which was established in the 18th century and now serves as a public archive. Further on, at Republic Street, lies the great siege square of the Turks, and not far from it is the National Library of Malta, with more than 60,000 books and manuscripts of the knights from different periods of its history.

On the corner of Republic Street, and the Old Theater street is Republic Square, which is considered the heart of the city. The square is surrounded by restaurants and cafés and has a monument to Queen Victoria. I continued on to the palace square which once belonged to the island governors and now houses the Parliament of Malta. From there I continued to gaze at the impressive Royal Opera House.

After several hours of wandering the city, I suddenly felt hungry. I went into one of the alleys and found a small local bakery, where the smell of the baked pastries enticed me to stop for a curious bite. I inquired the local baker as to what was the most recommended pastry in Malta. He suggested I try the local Pastizzi, a traditional savory pastry filled with cheeses or vegetables and lo and behold it just came out fresh of the hot oven! "Which do you prefer?" he asked me, "veggies or cheese?" "I'll have both," I answered with a smile, "why choose?"

I continued towards the Triq id-Dejqa street, where the young knights used to conduct battles, and during the British rule many bars and brothels were established at. After that I toured the Manoel Theater, which was established in the early 18th century and today it is a performing arts center. Further down the street is the Carmelite Church, whose dome rises to a height of 62 meters and it can be seen from every corner in Valletta.

Towards the end of my visit to Valletta, I stopped at a local

ice cream parlor, bought an ice cream cone made by the proprietors themselves, and headed for the Tritons Fountain, which is located near the entrance and exit gate to the city. As evening fell on Valletta the fountain was lit with bright colors. The fountain base was illuminated in yellow and orange while the three god statues were lit in deep blue and shades of green. I sat there for a while and enjoyed watching the people passing by. I love traveling the world. Some moments flood me with great happiness without any warning. That moment on the fountain was one of inexplicit happiness. I was delighted I had chosen to come to Malta and more importantly that I had another week to enjoy this island.

I went back to the hotel and showered, but I did not want my day to end. Since it was the season of the World Cup I decided to go out for a nice dinner and watch the game. The hotel clerk recommended the Cheeky Monkey Gastropub Qawra, located across from the hotel and was broadcasting the Mondial games.

I called Gil Lupo, my friend the film director I had met on the flight and invited him to have a drink and watch the game with me. Colombia played against Poland and the atmosphere at the pub was warming up. We got a great table near the television screen and sat on the rocking chairs that gave the place a special vibe. Next to us sat a group of tourists from Sweden who had also come to watch the game, and we started talking and had an amusing conversation late into the night. Four rounds of the local beer Cisk Lager and a very dramatic game that scored 3:0 in favor of country with the best coffee growers in the world, provided us with a very amusing evening.

Just before I returned to the hotel, I decided to walk on the promenade along the sea, enjoy the moonlight and the perfect weather. I walked towards the famous Malta National Aquarium which was a few hundred meters from the hotel, and when I got there and looked out towards the sea, I noticed the huge ship Hephaestus which ran aground in February 2018. The shipwreck remained as is for a long time because of the heavy costs of more than one million Euros required to tow it.

I continued walking towards the shipwreck and after about twenty minutes I reached it. I was there alone in the middle of the night and I felt completely unnerved by it. I faced that enormous ship and tried to imagine the volume of force that was needed to break the docking cables of this magnificent ship, which was more than 50 meters long and weighed about 880 tons, and smash it into one of Malta's deserted shores as if it were a weightless feather. I stood hypnotized and thought of the unimaginable story of the sinking of the Titanic and other stories of rescues and loss at sea. I looked at the dark Sea. It was so calm and quiet that I could not fathom its destructive powers. As I was standing there I remembered the days when I was in stormy waters, gliding through mighty waves and swimming in powerful currents. I thought about how the sea had taught me everything I knew in life and how its whirlwinds and ever-changing movement are some sort of a mirror to life.

DAY 2

A Motorcycle Adventure

*"You must not fight too often with one enemy,
or you will teach him all your art of war."*

- Napoleon Bonaparte

Having gone to bed so very late, I woke up later than usual to a dream about sailing at sea. My boat had capsized and was about to sink and just before I drowned I got rescued by a pod of dolphins. My imagination and mind were filled with my nighttime visit to the wrecked ship. For breakfast, I stopped at a little café and chose a traditional Malta breakfast of Sundried tomatoes, olives and Gozo cheese with freshly baked rolls.

That morning I decided to rent a motorcycle for the day through my hotel. Driving in Malta is on the left side of the road, and the last time I rode a motorcycle was in Greece, where they drive on the "right" side of the road, so I knew I had to pay close attention while riding the bike. The young man who brought the bike to me seemed worried for my safety, but I got on the motorcycle and took off quickly. After a couple of meters I stopped for a moment to put on my sunglasses and as I was looking back I saw that he was still watching me, only this time he was smiling and waving. I waved back and took off again.

My first adventure for the day was to ride the motorcycle to Saint Peter's Pool, which is a beautiful natural inlet pool located between Marsaxlokk fishing village and Delimara point and fort, on the south of Malta. The pool is deep and is surrounded by limestone rocks and cliffs. It is not a regular beach like the ones you find in most tourist destinations; this one had only the cliffs, the rocks, and the deep blue-green Mediterranean Sea waters. It is a favored diving area by divers, swimmers and snorkelers. During the peak summer months (the tourists' season), there are ladders available for swimmers to go down into the pool, but most travelers jump in and that is exactly what I did.

There are multiple heights to jump from, 10 feet to 20 feet, depending on your hesitance or boldness. I jumped from the highest rock and it was exhilarating. I then took a long swim in the beautiful clear sea water. When you swim in the pool, take your swim mask with you and explore the seafloor, as there are lovely rock formations in the area.

There are no beach chairs or any amenities at Saint Peter's pool since the pool is somewhat hidden, so be prepared to sit on the rocks if you want to sunbathe. After my swim, I sat on the limestone cliffs, sunbathing and watching the other travelers jump in and swim in the pristine turquoise water, listening to their excitement. I had a conversation with a nice couple from Canterbury, a small village in England, who had come to visit Valetta Island for the second time. It seems to be a recurring theme; Malta is not only a place for a one time visit but a location to which tourists keep coming back, especially the British. In fact, I remembered that Queen Elizabeth and her husband, the Duke of Edinburgh, had lived in Malta for a while before she became a queen. Years later, they both returned to Malta to celebrate their 60th anniversary.

I got on my motorcycle and rode to Marsaxlokk. It is a small fishing village known for its big fish market, which takes place around the whole village on Sundays, and for its many decorative colorful eye-painted boats called Luzzu and Kajjik. The village's name comes from the word Marsa, which means south-east (its location) in Maltese and is related to the dry sirocco wind that blows from the Sahara Desert south of it. The villagers are mostly fishermen.

I walked through the market, strolling among the local artifacts and merchandise like clothing, accessories, jewelry, food and art. The vibrant market looked colorful and picturesque with the backdrop of the ancient village with its old houses, palm trees, market stalls and, of course, the famous colorful fishing boats that docked in the blue sea, just like the images you see in the postcards.

When I got hungry I found a little coffee shop and bought another traditional Maltese food. This time, being in a fishing village, I tried a seafood dish platter with tuna, swordfish and calamari, sided with potato and a salad. It was delicious and very filling and I was surprised to see that the food in Malta is consistently good and very inexpensive. I sat for a while and watched people walking by.

After my meal, I bought a few things at the market; gifts and souvenirs, honey jars and beeswax and a hat to keep my head covered in the hot sun. I walked around the village and for a while, a local dog followed me around; it reminded me of Titti, Malta's cliff-diving dog, whom I watched on YouTube. This funny little brave dog is shown jumping into Saint Peter's pool, but only in exact timing with his owner.

While I was walking around the village I appreciated the different architectures each of Malta's occupiers left behind them. Walking in southern Malta streets, its buildings, homes and palm trees is a walk among memorandums of ancient Arabic culture.

Marsaxlokk church was looming large in the village. It was built as a fulfillment of a promise made by Marquess Rosalia Apap Viani Testaferrata after she was saved from a violent storm at sea. She dedicated the church to "our lady of the Rosary, the Madonna of Pompeii." On the last Sunday of July, the village celebrates the "Feast of Our Lady" with foods stands, a firework display and a procession carrying the statue of the Madonna.

I was tired of my wandering around the village and wanted to find a nice place by the water to watch the sunset. I sat in a little café I had found near the port and ordered a refreshing Aperol Spritz. The owner of the bar served me with my drink along with a warm welcome, and hung around my table for a short chat. He projected joie-de-vivre that is not easy to find everywhere. He told me of being the only person in his family who is not a fisherman and that he chose to be a restaurant owner despite the fact that it was frown upon in his fishermen family.

I looked at the view of the village harbor from the little coffee place. Some fishermen were busy repairing their nets, prepping the fish traps for their next day fishing trip and reconditioning the boats. They are never off from their job; either out at sea catching fish or maintaining their fishing boats.

I talked with the owner for a while about the boats and the history of the village. He was the third generation Maltese and his two brothers are still fishermen who sell their daily catch to big restaurants in Valletta. We talked about the national boats of Malta, the Luzzu and the Kajjik.

The luzzus are sturdy boats with a double-ended hull. Its design is believed to date back to Phoenician times and it survived because of its sturdiness and stability even in stormy seas. The word Luzzu comes from the Sicilian language and refers to a common fishing vessel used in Sicily. Originally, the Luzzu was equipped with sails but today almost all Luzzus are motorized with diesel engines.

The Luzzus are painted in bright colors of yellow, red, green and blues and the bow is traditionally painted with a pair of eyes. These painted eyes are a modern version of an ancient Phoenician custom and they are referred to as the Eye of Horus or of Osiris, both Egyptian deities, and as such they are said to protect the fishermen while at sea, ward off evil spirits and even tend to the boats while the owner is not present.

According to legend, the God Seth drowned Osiris, Horus' father, in the Nile River waters, dismembered his body into 14 pieces and scattered them along the Egyptian river. The beautiful goddess Isis, Osiris' wife, found all of her husband's remains, collected them and joined them back together, a gesture which gave Osiris a new life, though he remained in the underworld as the ruler of the dead and as a power that grants all life. It was believed that if you became one with Osiris' at death you would become immortal. Following Osiris resurrection, Isis gave birth to their son, Horus, therefore Horus was perceived as the representation of new beginnings by ancient Egyptians and The Eye of Horus symbolized sacrifice, healing, restoration and protection.

The pair of eyes painted on the Luzzus reminded me of the eye on the hand of Hamsa, a symbol that is a prominent fixture in many homes in Israel as well as on the doors of Arabic homes. The Hamsa is a sign of protection against the miserly, jealousy or evil gossip, and it is recognized throughout history as an amulet among the Jews, Muslims and Christians.

The Luzzu is often considered as a symbol of Malta. Some Luzzus have been converted into passenger carriers for tourists but most continue to be used as fishing vessels.

The Kajjik is similar in appearance and function to the luzzu, however, it is smaller and has a flat square stern instead of a double-ended hull. Kajjiks are also used in rowing races in Malta.

I learned some interesting customs from my very jovial and talkative host. For instance, when a fishing family member passes away, his name is marked on the Luzzu boat as a sign of respect and reverence for the dead.

We were communicating in English and I learned that Malta has two official languages, the Maltese language, which is mostly Semitic with a little Italian and Sicilian in it, and the English language, since Malta was a British colony for over 200 years. He taught me how to pronounce the name of the village correctly. Marsaxlokk is pronounced: Marsah-shlock, as the 'x' in Maltese sounds like the 'sh' in English. Most Maltese speak the Maltese language and English, and about half speaks Italian as well.

It was time for me to travel back, and I said my goodbyes and rode my motorcycle back heading towards the Saint Julian's area, as I wanted to explore the nightlife of Malta and this was the place to go to for bars, restaurants and entertainment.

I walked around the Saint Julian's area, which was brimming with tourists and locals mixing together in restaurants and bars. The hanging lights in each restaurant and around the Harbor made me feel as if I were a part of the festival, filled with vibrant sounds of laughter, music and locals and tourists' conversations.

Walking down one of the alleyways, I found a little restaurant/bar broadcasting the world cup football game on a big television screen; I went in and sat at the bar. I always love sitting at the bar, as the bartenders are the heart of the nightlife in each town I visited. I find them to be welcoming and always filled with stories, information and ideas on where to go and what to do in the city. They have inside information that they are always happy to share with the travelers. I watched the football game, had a beer and chatted with the people sitting on the stools next to me. They were traveling from Spain and I practiced my Spanish with them, talking about the World Cup and which team had a better chance to go all the way to the finals.

I wanted to go to a casino, so the bartender recommended the Dragonara Casino, which is located inside an old palace, right on the edge of the water. I am not much of a gambler, however, I wanted to see what it would be like to visit the casino, as it looked beautiful in photographs. The palace itself was built in 1870 and was used as a summer home for the Scicluna family. It is named after the Dragonara Peninsula on which it was built. Local legends tell the story of a dragon that lived in caves near the peninsula, but the growing heard by the locals was actually the sound of the waves hitting the rocks and the howling of the wind. I had heard that the TV series "Game of Thrones" filmed some of its scenes on that very peninsula and I thought it might be awesome to visit the location where they were filmed.

As I walked up the steps of the palace, I imagined what it was like for the family who lived there. During World War I, it was used as an officers' hospital and later, the family provided a home for refugees during World War II.

The palace opened as a casino in 1964 and was the first casino in Malta. It helped establish Malta as a tourist destination and it is still the most popular casino on the island. The palace was built in a neoclassical architecture with tall colonnades reminiscing the Italian grand style.

The grandeur of the palace was indeed striking, and the casino itself was beautiful and elegant and packed with people gambling away. I even tried my luck at a slot machine, but lady luck was not with me that night, though I was feeling very fortunate visiting this magical place.

I ended the day by going to the Grand Harbor to watch the famous Malta's fireworks. The international fireworks festival takes place in April and May and each year tourists from all over the world come just for this spectacular display. The fireworks seemed to be synchronized with the music playing in the background and the spectacle was breathtaking. The music and singing came from a floating stage in the majestic Grand Harbor.

It was a grand finale to a spectacular day of swimming in Saint Peter's pool, visiting the Marsaxlokk fishing village, enjoying the local markets, good food and people's hospitality, as well as visiting a beautiful casino and watching the fireworks on the grand harbor.

DAY 3

Gozo, Caves, Beaches & historical tale

"Once you have made up your mind, stick to it; there no longer any 'if' or 'but'."

- Napoleon Bonaparte

The next morning after riding the motorcycle the day before, I decided to do most of my sightseeing on foot. I had breakfast of Cheese Pastizzi (they are a bit addictive) with a strong coffee. I then headed to the Cirkewwa ferry, which was only 4 km away from my hotel and for a few Euros it can take you to the island of Gozo.

Gozo is the second largest island in Malta, on its north. The island's size covers about 67 square km with a population of 37,000 people.

Arriving in Gozo, I was struck by the different atmosphere it had, compared with the Maltese Island. It is more rural, with tranquility and calmness that I have not felt on its sibling southern island. I have read somewhere that locals in Gozo say that they operate on GMT, "Gozo maybe time".

Gozo is known for its peaceful scenic beaches, green landscapes, the prehistoric Ggantija temples, cobblestone streets and charming squares, old stone farmhouses, the Citadel, Baroque churches, century-old homes, spectacular coastline and luxury hotels. It has the best diving sites in Malta, but it is mostly known for being the home of the nymph Calypso, who detained Odysseus, the legendary Greek king of Ithaca and the hero of Homer's epic poem The Odyssey, on the island for seven years.

I got off the ferry at Mgarr Harbor, climbed up a hill and looked at the scenery of the bay below. I admired the striking landscape of the Citadel of Victoria, as it rises dramatically above the island and dominates the skyline.

Gozo is the perfect island for walking, as it is small and distances are minor. The roads are not busy and pleasant to walk on. There is a whole footpath network and I had my comfortable shoes on and an appetite for exploring Gozo. One of the local legends tells of a Gozitan wanderer who planted the Spanish Vetch plant all along the footpath so that hikers would not get lost.

I took the road towards the legendary Calypso cave, as I was fascinated by the story and wanted it to be my first stop on the island. I passed through a tranquil countryside with pretty houses and found my way to the cave-home of the nymph Calypso, which Homer wrote about in his Odyssey, the epic Greek poem of the 9th century B.C.

In Homer's tale the beautiful nymph Calypso, the daughter of the Titan Atlas, bewitches Odysseus and keeps him as a "prisoner of love" for 7 years, wanting to marry him and promising him immortality if he stayed. She enchants him with her singing as she weaves her loom with a golden shuttle. But Odysseus wants to go back and reunite with his wife, Penelope. Calypso reluctantly lets Odysseus go but only after Zeus sent Hermes to instruct her to release him. This story spoke to me as a reminder of the bewitching powers of the Maltese islands and reminded me of my beloved awaiting for me at home.

Though the cave itself is closed to the public, the view of the sea from the platform above it is stunning. The beautiful and most sought-after sandy beach of Ramla Bay, with its red sand, dominates the view. I took a path towards the beach where there were many tourists swimming and picnicking. It looked like it could be a great place for families as I saw lots of children playing in the soft reddish sand. From the beach I could see small coves and the unbelievable color of deep blue water of the sea.

I continued on walking for about thirty minutes to the prehistoric temples of Ggantija (Maltese for 'giant'), named so as the people of Gozo used to believe that the temples were built by a race of giants. Older than the pyramids of Egypt, the temples were erected during the Neolithic times, which makes these temples more than 5500 years old. They are one of the island main attractions and have been designated a UNESCO World Heritage site as the Megalithic Temples of Malta.

Walking around the huge and mysterious stone temples, I was moved by the sheer power of the ancient history of this place and even felt a soothing energy. There is evidence that the temples were used for ceremonial gatherings and perhaps rituals involving the sacrifice of animals. According to Gozo legend, a giantess who ate nothing but broad beans and honey bore a child of a common man. With the child hanging from her shoulder, she built these temples and used them as places of worship. It was powerful to walk around the huge stone structures at a place that was inhabited by ancient people and I was trying to comprehend as to how builders hauled these gigantic stones into place. Take your time walking around the temple and bring a hat in the summer, as there is almost no shade and the sun is hot. Luckily, when you are done with sightseeing, you can find your way to one of the nearest beaches on the island and enjoy a refreshing swim in the cool Mediterranean Sea.

I headed to Gozo's capital, Victoria. The name of the city was given to it by the British on the occasion of Queen Victoria's golden jubilee and it is also known as Rabat, especially by the older Gozitans. When I arrived at Victoria, I was tired and found a restaurant at the beautiful St. George Square. I sat down for a drink of Kinnie, which is a soft drink produced in Malta, because I heard it was the perfect beverage on a hot summer day. It had a bitter orange taste and I thought it would mix well with some Vodka, but I was saving that for the evening time, as I still had a lot to see in Gozo. I ordered Hobz biz-zejt, which is literally bread with oil and is a most common lunch dish. It is a sliced Maltese loaf of bread with extra virgin olive oil, balsamic vinegar, tomato paste and a pinch of salt and pepper, and I ordered it with tuna and capers.

In the heart of the city Victoria lays the Cittadella, a citadel which houses, among others, a cathedral, a museum, a science center, a war memorial and an old prison. The Cittadella is a castle, a fortress, and was the center of the island since the Bronze Age. The Knights of St. John reconstructed parts of the castle and for centuries the entire population of Gozo was required by law to spend the night within the Citadel for their own safety. In 1551, after repeated attacks by Turkish armies, the Citadel was overtaken and its citizens were taken into slavery. It took over 50 years to re-populate the island and rebuild the fortress. It was disturbing to think of an entire population taken by the Turks into slavery. Yes, that is what nations use to do at that time when winning a war, but my looking at where it took place and imagining the women and children, the horrors of war and slavery was unnerving, although it was beautiful and peaceful around me.

I walked around the narrow winding old streets, where I saw a church in almost every corner. In fact, for a small town, Victoria has many churches. I browsed the shops which sold Maltese Arts and Crafts. The pace of life here was indeed slow and I enjoyed the idleness of it all. I walked the Citadel and took photographs of the splendid city views.

Since Gozo is considered one of the top diving destinations in the Mediterranean, as well as being a center for water sports, I set my mind into going scuba diving and headed to the village of Xlendi on the south-west of the Gozo coast. The village has a Byzantine origin and is named after the Shilandi, an ancient galley ship that was wrecked along the coast. The old warship evidence was retrieved in 1960 and it became a known diving destination ever since.

Xlendi Bay is a popular swimming, snorkeling and diving spot. I walked the small sandy beach leading to the shallow waters that were perfect for the young and the old. For the more adventurous, it is great to swim and snorkel in deeper water off the long stretch of rocks bordering the beach. It is an ideal diving site because of its reef formations. There is also a small fishing village and good restaurants, bars and hotels. If you visit there for the day, and there are people with you who don't wish to go diving, they can dine at one of the restaurants, sunbath or sit at a café nearby while you are out diving.

It is also a perfect place to learn how to dive, as the water starts off very shallow and gradually deepens. There are boat dives for beginners, which include experts that guide while you are diving, and there are unaccompanied dives, for the skilled diver. I rented the equipment from a shop near the beach and headed for a dive with a private guide.

The water was incredibly clear and the landscape under the surface was so diverse. All the cracks, boulders, walls and caves created a varied and abundant fauna. My guide took me diving through small caves and caverns, where the visibility was excellent. There was a moment when I was surrounded by a school of redfish, observing me as they spun all around me. I felt as if I was one of them and belong in their ecosystem. At that moment, a sheer delight overcame me; these are the moments I live for, moments of exploring new terrains and discovering the joy of adventures.

The experience of diving calms me and I always enjoy looking for the balance between floating and falling. There is one moment of perfect balance in which you are in complete equilibrium and become one with the sea. At these moments I even forget that I need to breathe and as in fairy tales, I become a true son of the sea.

Before I went diving, I spoke with a couple who suggested I climb the steps up the side of the cliffs, to a concrete bench seat part where they liked to sit and enjoy the peace and the views, while watching everything that was going on below. I followed their advice and went to the beautiful spot after my long dive and enjoyed the spectacular views of the bay and the cliffs above. From up above, where I was sitting, I could see some of the caves and remembered the story of the Caroline Cave, situated on the right of the bay. It was once the property of Caroline Cauchi, a rich unmarried woman from Victoria, whose life mission was to build a monastery in Gozo. She later founded the Augustinian Sisters Order and donated her land, including the cave and other lands in Xlendi to the monastery. The nuns started staying there in the summers. They would go for a swim in the isolated cave which could only be reached by stairs, so it was their own private pool, and would not be seen by other people in the bay. The cave is well known for its clear blue water.

I decided to end the day enjoying a meal at Ta Karolina restaurant, situated just before the steps leading to Karolina cave. I sat outside under the awning and enjoyed the home-made ravioli stuffed with Gozo cheese. I ate and sipped my Kinnie cocktail while the sun began to set. As it was getting dark, the hanging lights at the restaurant lit and it felt like a very magical romantic place to be at.

The evening was descending. I was tired and ready to get back to my hotel on Malta. This time I took a taxi to Mgarr for the ferry back to Cirkewwa on Malta. The ferry ride was quick and after a long day of sightseeing and lots of hiking, I took a shower and fell asleep right away.

DAY 4

Sailing to the Blue Lagoon

"Nothing is more difficult, and therefore more precious, than to be able to decide."

- Napoleon Bonaparte

I woke up the next morning excited for a new adventure. I was meeting up with my friend Gil and some of his film crew to go yachting and sailing for the day. I had an English breakfast at a little café, a typical Malta breakfast of fried eggs, potatoes, tomatoes, that came with a small bowl of beans and toast. I was watching the wonderful sea views from the café while I was eating. The weather was beautiful as it was every day since I got here and the sea seemed calm and perfect for spending the day on a boat.

Yachting in Malta is very popular, as yacht owners find the weather in Malta and its location in the center of the Mediterranean, with its beautiful natural harbors, incredibly desirable. The accessibility to all of Europe's marinas and the facilities for boats make it a natural choice for all boating.

Some say that yachting existed in Malta as far back as 1835, but only in 1896 a small group started the first Malta Sailing Club, which was mostly for cruising. This became a racing venue that attracted other sailing enthusiasts. After World War II, 'The Malta Royal Yacht Club' was formed and racing to various places such as Sicily, Libya and Tunisia resumed regularly. In 1968, the first Middle Sea Race set sail and became a premier international event. In 1987, the Rimini-Malta-Rimini race began. There is also an annual race from Malta to Tunisia, a country to which I hope to travel one day.

If you are a licensed skipper you can charter a boat through one of the private companies in Malta. If you are looking for a fun place to hang out, drink and meet other sailors from around the world, the Royal Malta Yacht club is the place for you. It is also a place where you can take a shower after a cruise, have a meal and use of the Wi-Fi service.

I met up with Gil and the three of his film crew and we headed towards the Cirkewwa Ferry. A big handheld sign greeted us at the parking lot and the woman holding it was Ann from the Charter Company. Ann smiled and introduced herself to us and together we walked towards the marina where her husband and partner, Andy, were waiting. We chose to hire them because their company, "Lust for Life Day Charters in Malta," received great reviews and many recommendations on Facebook.

We boarded the medium size yacht and headed north. The

yacht was very similar to a boat I sailed around the Greek Islands a few years ago. We were going on a boat ride around the islands of Malta and the highlight of our sail was to visit the lighthouse on the island of Gozo.

I have a bit of a fascination and a great fondness for lighthouses, as they represent such a magical and historical narrative of light and hope at sea. It is admirable that the man in the lighthouse dwells in the total darkness of the ocean surrounds him, and all by himself he marks the way for ships to navigate while in the ocean, provides safe entries and assists in finding direction. I am always on the lookout for lighthouses in my travels all over the world and today is another one of these special trips to go see the lighthouse in Gozo, close-up.

The yacht steered smoothly in the Mediterranean Sea and we were soon rounding the island of Comino, entering the Blue Lagoon. From the sea I could see the landscape of Comino and the lagoon. We anchored and got into the water for a swim and snorkeling on the lagoon's reef. Andy inflated a huge pink flamingo water float and threw it overboard. We all jumped after it, floated on it sunbathing and squealing in delight. After the blue lagoon swim, we continued on with our sail around the island and stopped at a couple of lagoons where I took pictures of the caves and cliffs. The landscape of Malta from the sea is astounding; ancient cliffs, rocks, towns and the forever blue sea.

Andy and Ann prepared a beautiful meal for us on the boat, including bread, cheese, beer and cocktails. We ate and drank and chatted with them to learn about their story. Andy was a businessman and Ann a lawyer, living in Germany; they were very successful in their profession, hence they were always very busy. Eventually, they found themselves very tired of their stressful lifestyle. Though their great financial rewards were very enticing and kept them going for a while, they realized one day that they were fed up of that "rat race" and decided to leave it all behind. They sold their house in Germany and bought a small house on the magical island of Gozo, as well as a boat that will accommodate their new lifestyle, and they moved to Malta full time.

They lived a quiet life on the small island in the middle of the Mediterranean, and started taking tourists on daylong trips, sailing around the island. That is how their business started. They usually take a group of people for yachting and sailing. It was amazing to be on their yacht and be inspired by this young couple's brave decision to leave their jobs and stress behind and live their dream life of fewer work hours, less stress, drinking beer in the middle of the sea with their clients while earning their livelihood. After a few cocktails, we swam and snorkeled, and finally, we headed towards the Gozitan landmark.

The Giordan Lighthouse, or as it is called in Maltese Ta' Gurdan, is an active lighthouse located on a hill above the village of Ghasri in northern Gozo. It can be seen for twenty nautical miles, and its light flashes every 7.5 seconds.

The lighthouse was built during the British Empire rule in Malta, to help meet the needs of the increasing maritime traffic around Malta. During WWII, it was used as a warning radar station that provided information about bombers flying south from Italy. Its early warnings activated sirens that helped the residents get to safety on time. Originally, the lighthouse had twenty one oil lamps, seven on each of its three sides. The brass reflectors were silver plated and made the beam visible a full thirty eight miles away.

The lighthouse is a main tourist attraction and provides a panoramic view across the island of Malta. You can reach it by walking up the steep hill from the village. If the lighthouse attendant is on the premises, he might let you take a look inside and perhaps allow you to climb the spiral staircase to the top of the lighthouse. If he is not around, you can walk around the top of the hill where there are ruins of a colonial military observation post. On a clear day, you can see Sicily in the north, as the breeze cools you down after the steep climb.

Lighthouses were once regarded as an unconditional service to the public, meaning ships could benefit from the light and assistance in navigation they provided, without being forced to pay for entering into a harbor.

Along the way to Gozo there is a lot of activity in the water. We encountered fishing vessels dropping nets and Tankers traveling south with their cargo, to the north coast of Africa, or returning from Sicily, or further north. I took a yacht cruising course a few years ago and I have been sailing around the world ever since. Andy let me navigate when we stopped the engine to enjoy a little wind sailing the sails up. With the engine off it was quieter on the boat and each of us took time to himself to breathe in the smell of the open ocean, to enjoy the views and the delicate rocking of the boat by the waves.

There is only one official Marina on the island of Gozo, but there are plenty of sheltered bays, perfect for dropping anchor and spending a couple of hours swimming in the clear water, or enjoying a meal and wine aboard the boat. There are many guided boat trips with local charter companies using speedboats, yachts or converted fishing boats, and the prices are very reasonable. Some vacationers in Malta charter a boat for a week or longer. Listening to Andy talk about chartering a boat for a whole week, I thought it would be an amazing trip to do one day and how I was very much suited for spending a full week on a yacht in Malta, as I love sailing and being at sea. The sailing season in Malta is long and stretches from May to October.

I could already see the cliffs of Gozo, with their many caves, and on top of the green hill sat the Ta Jordan lighthouse of Gozo. Chills went down my spine as I imagined the countless ships and boats that this beacon led to safety on stormy nights, the hope and courage it brought to sailors and the relief mariners felt when they saw its light shining in the darkness.

If you haven't had a chance to sail or cruise on a yacht before, do find a way to do so, as I believe everybody needs to experience it at least once. It felt tremendous to be on a boat in the middle of the Mediterranean Sea, at the crossroads that had seen ancient civilizations, wars, famine and the development of Christianity in this part of the world. Sailing on a sailboat is like entering a time machine that takes you back to a time when people were navigating by the stars and tides. I imagined the courage that people had going out to sea on a mission to discover the unknown.

We stopped at a little cove near the village of Ghasri and I jumped in the crystal clear water to swim and splash and to explore the reef with my snorkeling mask. The natural beauty was breathtaking. The small beach was perfect for a stroll and a picnic. I took out my trusted sketchbook to sketch for a little bit, eating some snacks prepared by Andy and Ann, while Gil and his crew shot a video of the island.

Our day was winding down and we headed back to Malta tired but content, as we were all going to the 'Isle of MTV' music festival that evening. We said our goodbyes to Andy and Ann and got back to the hotel for a quick dinner with friends before the show.

Nearly 50,000 people go to the Isle of MTV early in the

afternoon just to get a place near the stage. If you prefer to see the musical acts up close, you should try to get there by 3 PM even though the festival itself starts later. While I love the music of Jason Derulo, who was headlining the festival, I was a little tired from a full day of sailing, being under the sun, and swimming in the sea, so it wasn't that important for me to arrive early and wait for hours until the show began.

The Isle of MTV–one of the most entertaining events to take place in Malta–is the annual music festival organized by MTV Europe. The festival has been held in Malta since 2007, though previous versions were hosted by Portugal, France, Spain and Italy. Organized annually on a day in either June or July, it begins at 6 PM and ends by midnight. It is free and there are no age limits to enter, so youngsters from all over Malta and Gozo join adults and European tourists to enjoy the show at the open air Granaries in Floriana. Special buses run to and from the festival. In the latest editions, almost 50,000 people attended, popularizing it as the biggest free music festival around. Therefore, make sure you register early for the concert as it fills up quickly.

Floriana is a fortified town just outside the capital city Valletta. The Granaries themselves are pits dug into the ground and covered with round stone slabs. They were used to store grain and can be found throughout Valletta and Floriana. First built by the Knights to provide storage in the event of a siege, the British eventually copied all details of the Knights' granaries and used them to provide grain for the

population during World War II. The Granaries at Floriana are now officially named Pjazza San Pulju, which is also known as the largest urban open space in Malta, used primarily for mass gatherings. When John Paul II visited Malta in 1990, it was here that people came to see and hear him. In 2001, three Maltese were sanctified during the second Papal visit in the plaza, and since Malta is a mostly Catholic country, this was considered a monumental event.

We got to the plaza at 9 PM to find the square already full. We stood by the St. Publius Parish Church, on the other side from the stage. The atmosphere was filled with fun and excitement. I heard many languages spoken and lots of laughter; people were taking pictures and videos of the square, the buildings surrounding it and the granaries. A group of young teenagers walked by me, speaking Maltese while laughing happily. The pre-program started with several Maltese singers performing. There were cheers and excitement, and though I did not know the singers and bands, the rhythm and beat were great, and the applause they got from their Maltese countrymen told me that they were very well known in Malta.

The musical line-up this year included the great Jason Derulo, a US pop and R&B artist who already sold over 30 million singles. He rocked the plaza with his performance. His singing, the dancers on the stage, the crowds around me, and all of us dancing to the beat felt truly special. The colors of the shimmering lights changed with the beat and made it all look magical. The beautiful Hailee Steinfeld, who first achieved fame as an Oscar-nominated actress, sang songs from her debut platinum album, and she and her dancers roused the audience to a frenzy. British house DJ and producer Sigala performed his hit single Easy Love and got the audience pumped up for the release of his new album. The beautiful dancers on the stage were spectacular, and people all around us rocked to the music, dancing, drinking beers, sharing laughter and joyfulness. The festival also featured live vocals from Paloma Faith, Ella Eyre, and DJ dance duo Dimitri Vegas & Like Mike. The audience sang and danced to the music all night long.

At a certain point, the revelry, the dancing, and drinking reached a whirling, feverish moment of musical ecstasy, and Gil, the women, and I all had a blast, partying as if we were celebrating life itself. As evening and darkness descended, the square was packed with happy music lovers, illuminated by beams of differently colored shimmering lights. At some moments the square was aglow in purple, at other times red and blue. I moved my body to the beat and felt the exhilaration that only music brings out of me.

I knew how far-reaching this concert was; among the artists who performed in the past few years were: Lady Gaga, Rita Ora, Flo Rida, Kid Rock, Snoop Dogg, the Black Eyed Peas, Nelly Furtado, Maroon 5, and Enrique Iglesias, all on the same Isle of MTV stage. My instincts to come to Malta and experience it for myself were spot on.

I was also delighted with the fact that the Isle of MTV music festival is giving music lovers an incentive to visit Malta, and is expanding the country's mix of tourists by attracting younger people to the Island.

Being a famous director, Gil was well-connected and knew some of the organizers. He took us backstage where we met the MTV dancers and visited the studios. We saw the structures where all the computers and TV monitors were set up to stream the festival on television and the Internet. It was exciting to see how it was all filmed and streamed live for audiences all over Europe.

The partying carried on late into the night. Afterward, we took a big taxi and did not get back to the hotel until three in the morning—I fell asleep with my clothes on. I felt so thrilled to have been a part of this music festival, on this island of Knights and sun. This was indeed the party of the summer.

DAY 5

A Walking Tour on Comino Island

"Until you spread your wings, you'll have no idea how far you can fly."

- Napoleon Bonaparte

Getting up late the next morning, I headed to the Cirkewwa ferry, which I took to Comino, a small island situated between Malta and Gozo in the Mediterranean Sea. Comino is only 3.5 square kilometers in area. The ferry was quick; I was there within 35 minutes. I wanted to experience the island on foot, even though I already saw it from the sea.

The island is the least populated area in the Republic of Malta and only has three permanent residents following the death of the fourth resident in 2017. As the ferry approached the island, I could see the rugged and rocky coastline with its limestone cliffs, the small sandy beaches, coves, and a shoreline dotted with caves.

Comino is named after the cumin seed that once flourished on the Maltese islands. It has a bird sanctuary and a nature preserve, and serves as a paradise for snorkelers, divers, windsurfers and hikers. Almost uninhabited, it is car-free and has only one hotel. There is also only one priest and one policeman, both of whom commute from the island of Gozo.

When the Knights of Malta arrived on the island, they used Comino as recreational and hunting grounds, as well as a staging post in the defense against the Ottoman Empire. The Knights were protective of the wild game on the island, which was abundant with wild boar and hares. If an unlawful hunter was convicted, he was harshly penalized by serving three years as a galley slave. Comino was also where Knights were imprisoned for minor crimes, or at other times, they were sentenced to the dangerous task of manning Saint Mary's Tower. During the French occupation, Comino was used to quarantine the very sick.

Legend states that 700 years ago, a quiet, God-loving holy man named Kerrew was driven out of his home in Malta by less spiritual neighbors who did not understand nor like his God-fearing ways. His tormentors pursued him to the coast, but his mystical powers allowed him to cross the sea to Comino while laying a curse on his pursuers. He stayed for some time on the island, where he befriended a hermit and mystic by the name of Abulafia. Eventually, he moved to a cave in Gozo, where he lived for the rest of his life. Kerrew's curse indeed came true: Malta was hit by a plague, attacked by Muslim Corsairs, and besieged by the Turks. Although Malta survived the siege and triumphed, it suffered heavy losses. The legend of Kerrew still lives on, and some claim they can see his resurrected body crossing over to Comino, just to have a chat with Abulafia.

In truth, from 1285 to 1290, Comino was the home of exiled Jewish Prophet and Kabbalist Abraham Abulafia. It was on this island that Abulafia composed The Book of the Sign, and his last work, Words of Beauty. A mystic ahead of his time, he dreamt of unifying Judaism, Islam and Christianity into one religion. Abulafia might have been the founder of modern practical Kabbalah. I heard that in the Jewish community in Malta, lives an elderly man known to all as "The Admor," who claims to be a direct descendant of the hermit.

In the 1960's, tourists rediscovered and revived Comino. It is perfect for people seeking a very tranquil vacation.

The island's main attraction is the world-renowned Blue Lagoon, and I headed there when I arrived on the ferry. A sheltered inlet that lies in the stretch of water between Comino and the tiny uninhabited island of Cominotto, it boasts of a brilliant, crystal-clear, azure-colored seawater, and a seafloor consisting of brilliant, almost-white sand.

The lagoon is very popular with day-trippers, serving as a meeting place for all kinds of boats, ranging from ten-footers to sixty-foot yachts, who come from the main island to spend the day at this picturesque beach. It is also famous for its underwater beauty and considered a diver's paradise.

I jumped into the water and took a long swim in the beautiful bay. It was still early in the morning and not very busy, as the boats had not yet arrived to make the place more crowded. The lagoon itself is cordoned off so that swimmers could swim safely and snorkelers could freely observe the marine life found in this area.

After my swim, I decided to explore the island and come back to the Blue Lagoon before finally returning to Malta. I headed north towards the only hotel on the island, the Comino Hotel and Bungalows. The hotel sports a pinkish hue that fits perfectly into the environment of the island. It has swimming pools and a private beach. Situated on the San Niklaw Bay and providing an incredible view of the sea, the hotel is popular with tourists and Maltese alike. I stopped by the hotel lobby bar for a strong espresso and chatted with the server about his work. He told me that he lives in Gozo but likes coming in daily to work on Comino, as he enjoys the island's beauty and calm. He is an amateur photographer, so during the winter when the hotel is closed, he comes to the island to take photographs of the landscape. I thought that one day I would love to come back to Comino in winter, as it would be a sight to behold.

I continued walking towards the Santa Maria Bay and caves. I stopped occasionally to take in the views and observe nature. The island is quite bare, with just a few trees, the breathtaking cliffs and the Mediterranean. As I went on my way, I could see the deep caves on the side of the cliffs.

Under the hot sun, these caves can offer shelter.

Santa Maria Bay is located on the north side of Comino, and after the Blue Lagoon, it is the second best place for picnics and swimming. The beach is lovely and the water great for snorkeling and scuba diving. The Comino Hotel bungalows are located at the bay, and there is even a campsite. I found it quiet and very peaceful. If you prefer more of a beach feel, you could reserve sunbeds on this beach to sunbathe in comfort, while occasionally going for a swim or snorkeling.

Feeling hungry, I found a food cart and ordered a feta salad sandwich on traditional Gozitan bread. I sat on the sand and ate while gazing at the dramatic cliffs sloping into the aquamarine water. There were only a handful of people around, giving the place very meditative feel, so I sat there drawing in the sketchbook I take with me everywhere.

I like to draw objects in motion: birds, boats, animals, and so on. To do that, I relied on quick observation skills to "catch" the subject's essence and then turn it into lines and drawings. That is how I stretch my drawing abilities. A bird in flight moves continuously, so when you sketch it, the angle you see changes from moment to moment. You must first capture the image in your memory, then translate that memory immediately into the sketchbook.

Drawing is a therapeutic and relaxing experience, and I lose all sense of time when I draw. I suggest you bring a notebook or a sketchpad along on your travels and try to draw things you see on your trip. It is a very enjoyable, creative experience that reinforces many skills and can help you improve in many areas. I drew some picturesque sketches of boats against the vistas of the Mediterranean Sea and the cliffs of Malta, as well as drawings of seagulls standing on a rock near me.

The Santa Maria Caves provide interesting dives for all levels. If you are an underwater photographer, you will be able to take stunning pictures of aquatic life. There are ten caves known to divers, each with their own particular beauty. Some offer great swimming spots, others have large underwater tunnels, while others provide fascinating views. The caves are shallow, and some of them are partially above water.

The caves provide the perfect spot for snorkelers, so I put on my gear and dove in. The reef presented me with views of gorgeous marine life: I saw an octopus, crabs, spiny lobsters, eels, damselfish, and the eel-like morays. A snorkeler next to me was feeding bread to a Banded Sea Bream, and I watched as the fish swarmed all around him in a great swirl. I felt the power and peace of the water, and the feeling of being one with nature once more.

After leaving the caves, I continued on my walk, this time heading to Saint Mary's Tower, located across the island from the Santa Maria Bay. I hiked past pine trees and through a valley filled with buzzing bees, colorful butterflies, and the chirping and singing of birds. As I walked, I could smell the scent of the wild thyme in the air, and I imagined being a farmer during Roman times, working in the fields under the hot sun.

Saint Mary's is a large bastioned watchtower and stands as the most prominent structure on the island. I even saw it from the ferry on my way over. The tower was built in 1618 by the Knights of Malta as part of a connective chain of towers all along the coast of the Maltese islands. It was meant to defend Comino from Ottoman pirates who attacked ships traveling between Malta and Gozo. In case of an attack, it also served as a communications link between the two main islands of Malta, as the Knights were determined to defend the channel between the islands.

The building is a massive square structure that juts up 80 meters above sea level, with four corner turrets built on a huge stone platform. There is a prominent semi-circular gun platform facing the sea. Malta's national trust restored it extensively in the last few years. I had to climb many steps to reach the top, but it was well worth it as the views from atop the tower are spectacular.

On the way back towards the ferry, I stopped by the Crystal Lagoon, a less well-known location with emerald green water that is as beautiful as the Blue Lagoon's. The cliffs are high and there are boats that come to this place so tourists can swim and cool off in the sea. I watched as the occasional tourist jumped into the water from the high cliff, but most just hiked by or sat around enjoying the view.

I got to the ferry, took one last look at the Blue Lagoon, and headed back to Malta, very happy and satisfied with my full day of exploring Comino Island. I got dinner at an Indian restaurant near my hotel then sat on the balcony to view the water. Indian food always differs depending on where you are in the world. The kitchen was open and I could see my food being cooked, with the owner overseeing everything. It was fresh and delicious. Satisfied, I headed back to the hotel for a good night's rest before my next day's adventure in Malta.

DAY 6

The Western Secrets of Malta

"The stupid speak of the past, the wise of the present, and fools of the future."

- Napoleon Bonaparte

On my 6th day, I wanted to visit the small village of Manikata in the northwestern part of the island. It is a typical Maltese rural village, close to the seaside, and is ideal for walking and enjoying the locality. Many tourists visit this village all year round. The word "Manikata" is derived from the Italian word "Manica," which means sleeve. From my hotel, I rode a taxi across the island and within 15 minutes arrived at the village. The landscape reminded me of how I imagined Malta existed before modern times.

The village's main industry is farming and it oversees the farming in the valley around it. There are 40 families in the village, totaling into a population of about 600 people. The abundant and rich produce from the fields include grapes, tomatoes, potatoes, onions, melons, apples, oranges, pome-granates, and many other crops that Manikata provides to

the tourist industry on the island. There are also many bee-keepers in the area.

There are structures reminiscent of the different occupiers of the island and the different periods in history. Seeing many cart ruts that date back from the Bronze Age, I followed one trail the long way from under a tree, towards the parish church, until it ended at the cliffs. There are also many Bronze Age defensive walls around the village, some 8 meters tall. This is characteristic of that period, where a village would be built on a hill and surrounded with defensive walls to protect it against their enemies.

I walked through the ancient Roman tombs near Manikata. Farmers have wrecked some of these tombs to create space for their fields; other tombs are found in caves and have been used for different purposes by later inhabitants. Some of these tombs were used as air raid shelters during World War II. In some instances, nature, trees and vegetation have taken over the old burial chambers. There are remains of Roman baths, some still holding while others crumbling.

In the Middle Ages, the farmers lived in the caves around Manikata alongside their livestock, cultivating crops and fruit trees through the fields that belonged to landowners from the capital.

During the Knights of St. John's time, the Turkish fleet dropped anchor on the bays around Manikata and launched their attack on Birgu. At the time, Birgu was the headquarters of the Knight's Order. Subsequently, the Grand Masters of the Knights built watchtowers on the cliffs, Saint Agatha's Tower and coastal entrenchments to prevent enemy troops from landing on the sandy beach.

Ghajn Tuffieha Tower was built in 1637 on the cliffs of Ghajn Tuffieha Bay. It is one of the seven towers built by Grand Master Lascaris, during the times of the Knights of Malta. A tall tower, it was armed with a cannon and usually manned by four men.

During the British period on Malta, many farmers in Manikata lost agricultural land, which was taken over by the British for the construction of a Royal Marines Training Center. During WWI, the center was used as a military hospital for wounded soldiers and employed nurses from Manikata.

When Mussolini invaded Ethiopia in 1935, the British built coastal defenses--called beach posts--out of concrete, and camouflaged with rubble walls to defend against the possibility of an invasion. Two of these beach posts were built on Manikata. During WWII, more beach posts were built along the coast and were provided with a searchlight in order to spot enemy aircraft. The village was often a target during air raids due to the presence of the Admiralty camp. The residents took shelter in caves and the Roman tombs.

Today the people who come to live in Manikata dwell in

serene and beautiful surroundings. Many of the villagers are farmers. The people I saw on my walk were warm and welcoming in the typical Mediterranean way, proud of their culture and of their island. I realized that Malta is not a melting pot of cultures introduced by foreign empires, but rather there is a foundation of age-old traditions, customs, and values passed on through generations of Maltese families unrelated to the culture left by foreign rule. The most evident of these values is their pride in being Maltese.

The Old Chapel of St. Joseph was built in 1920 when there were only twelve families living in Manikata. The families built the honey-colored stone church; some can still recall how the stones and the arches were brought to the village. Since it became too small for the needs of the village, a new church was commissioned and built, and finally completed in 1974. The architect of the church took his inspiration from the "girna," a small stone building put up by farmers to store their tools in the middle of the field.

Every last Sunday in August, the parish celebrates the Feast of St. Joseph. The night before the feast, the community celebrates the Summer Breeze Night, which includes a talent show, drama, art, food, honey and wine.

Walking through the village, I saw many stone buildings with fossilized seashells embedded into the rocky surface. I learned that most Maltese masonry buildings are construct-ed from softer granite, giving the country its characteristic

golden hue. Geologically, there are three main rock layers. The bottom is the Coralline limestone, which consists of sand and gravel mixed with shell fossils. It is hard, resistant to erosion, and forms the steep, vertical cliffs along the coast. The middle rock is the soft limestone, which is the building stone. Finally, above it lies the thin Blue Clay, Malta's softest rock, which is impermeable.

After walking through the village, I wanted to visit the beaches around it. I first headed to Ghajn Tuffiena Bay, which translates into "Apple's spring." I walked down the 189 steps leading to the bay and took a stroll around the white stretch of sandy beach. There were many local families enjoying picnics and sunbathing. You can rent sunbeds and sun umbrellas if you come for the day, and enjoy the picturesque quiet beach, swimming and windsurfing.

The water was shallow at first, but I walked out into the deep and swam in the aquamarine and emerald sea. It felt a bit like an earthly paradise.

After my swim, I headed to a beach bar at the edge of the bay. I sat on the terrace, had a sparkling Kinnie, and tried a Lampuki pie, which is a baked pastry with fish. I enjoyed the delicious dish, which was inexpensive and quickly served. When I was done eating, I burned off the calories by walking back up the 189 steps.

Next, I visited Golden Bay, another beach near Manikata. It

is located along unspoiled and undeveloped countryside; there are small pebbles at the edge of the water, so bring water shoes if you want to go swimming. The water can be rough at times, and the currents strong. When the red flag is up, swimming is limited to shallow waters because of the underwater currents from the Northwest winds.

I heard that Golden Bay is one of the best places to watch the sunsets, as the water shimmers when the sun hits the horizon. I thought of my girlfriend back home. This could be an amazing romantic spot to bring her to.

In fact, the breathtaking landscapes of Malta have been immortalized in movies and shows, and you could come across some locations and scenery while visiting the island. One of my favorite television series, Game of Thrones, shot some scenes in Manikata, specifically the episode named "The Pointy End" where the Dothraki attacked a village and Kahl Drogo is wounded. I like discovering the shooting locations of known films and TV series. The fact that these locations have been celebrated on film makes the atmosphere even more magical.

Next, I took a short taxi ride to Popeye's Village, north of Manikata. It was built as a film set for the production of the 1979 film Popeye. It has since grown into one of the major tourist attractions on the Maltese Islands, with fun activities for the young and the young at heart.

Having loved animation from a very young age, I grew up watching all the Popeye cartoons, which were based on E.C. Segar's comic strips. The childhood memories of these cartoons--Popeye eating spinach and becoming all-powerful--are still present in my love for eating anything with spinach in it. Spinach still makes me feel strong and invincible. I was very excited to experience this park and tour the village for a few hours. It is open all year round, and has an open-air museum as well as being a seaside resort.

The film production company took seven months to build the village set, which has 19 wooden buildings. Some materials were imported from the Netherlands and Canada. Once the set was ready, filming began in January 1980 (when I was two years old), and wrapped in June of that same year.

Besides the film sets, there are many family attractions to experience: shows, rides, museums and playhouses where children can climb and explore the village and meet the main characters from the show.

Animated films and shows influenced me in such a way that when I got older, I studied animation, art and painting. Today, drawing, creating characters and storytelling encompass who I am. Walking around in a place that made an animated show and its cartoon characters come to life brought great joy in me. I became like a child again and had a fantastic time in the village.

Before I left, I took a 20-minute solitary boat trip around Anchor Bay and watched families with their excited children do the same. I took amazing photographs of the Popeye Village from the sea. In the center of the village, there is a complex where visitors can view a 20-minute show on the history of the village, which includes scenes from the film. The village hosts many functions and activities, including lunches, dinners and offering the village as a dream-wedding venue.

There are performers providing entertainment for families, including an interactive puppet show, the Barber of Seville singing opera while creating artistic hairstyles, and a song and dance play about Popeye and his friends.

Since I was close to Saint Agatha's Tower, I headed there to watch the sunset, as I heard it is a beautiful spot for it. Also known as the Red Tower, it is a large bastioned watchtower in Mellieha. It was built in 1647 and was the last large bastioned tower to be erected in Malta. The structure consists of a square tower with four corner towers. There are cannon ports in the turrets, the outer walls are four meters thick, and a barrel-vaulted roof encloses the tower's interior. A chapel is located inside the building.

The tower is situated in a commanding position on the crest of the Marfa Ridge on the northwest end of Malta, overlooking potential enemy landing site of Mellieha Bay. It has clear views of the islands of Comino and Gozo, as well of the line of watchtowers to the east, along the north shore of Malta that linked it with the Knights headquarters in Valletta. As it was the Knights' primary stronghold in the west of Malta, I was very curious to visit it.

There was a troop of 30 men stationed in the fortress, with ammunition and supplies to withstand a siege of 40 days. The idea of getting besieged in this tower, and the bravery the men who protected it, was horrifying to think about. During the British period on Malta, the Red Tower continued to have a military function, and was in use during both WWI and WWII. The Armed Forces of Malta used it as a radar station. The strategic importance of this tower is very evident when you visit it, and it is fascinating for children as well. The tower was extensively restored and is now open to the public.

A very knowledgeable guide took me on a tour around the tower, and the panoramic view of Gozo and Comino from the top was splendid. There are sunset tours and a glass of wine upon admission. If marriage is on your mind, this is a beautiful place for it.

I watched the sunset with a glass of Maltese wine in hand, toasting with the other tourists around me as we enjoyed a magical moment together. It was such an exciting day full of activities, and after sunset, I returned to my hotel, had a quick dinner, and fell rapidly asleep.

DAY 7

Feeling like a movie star for the day

"If you want a thing done well, do it yourself."

- Napoleon Bonaparte

The island of Malta has served as a film location since 1925, and there have been over 110 movies and shows filmed here. Many dramas, documentaries, and television series have used the dramatic backdrop of the cliffs, the ancient landscape, and the Mediterranean Sea. In a way, they added another character to the story: the island of Malta itself.

Besides the Popeye set that I visited yesterday, the list of films includes: Midnight Express, The Count of Monte Cristo, U-571, Gladiator, and Simshar, which you might not be familiar with but it was shot entirely in Malta, using mostly Maltese actors and the Maltese language. It is based on a true story of a shipping boat that goes missing with its crew, a real tragedy that happened in Malta in 2008. Other known films shot in Malta are Captain Phillips, Troy, and the James Bond movie, The Spy Who Loved Me.

Game of Thrones also filmed in the walled city of Mdina, which doubled as King's Landing. The island's forts served as the Red Keep, and the stunning natural arch knows as the Azure Window in Gozo was the setting for Khal Drogo and Daenerys Targaryen's wedding.

On my last day on the island, I decided to visit the city of Mdina to see the locations where the first season of Game of Thrones was filmed.

The history of Mdina is extensive and goes back more than 4,000 years. It is said that the Apostle St. Paul lived in the town after being shipwrecked on the islands. St. Paul converted the Roman governor to Christianity after miraculously healing his father, then converted the local population to Christianity, making the Maltese some of the earliest Christians and the island a Christian state.

Mdina is referred to as "the Silent City." It is fascinating to visit for the ancient atmosphere, its medieval and baroque architecture, and the cultural and religious treasures, as well as being a perfect example of an ancient European walled city.

As I entered through the main gate of the walled city, I walked down the same path that Game of Thrones characters did on the show. It was here where Catelyn rode into King's Landing, and where the farewell scene between Ned Stark and Catelyn took place when she left King's Landing after the death of King Robert. I continued walking for a few minutes before arriving at Mesquita Square, which was the setting for many scenes including the one where Jamie Lannister and his spearmen attack Ned Stark and his guards. It is also the setting for the trellised balcony of Petyr Baelish's bordello. The square was quiet and unassuming as I walked through it in the sunlight.

I continued strolling through the city and watched a black-clad priest passing me by with his head bowed. The streets were mostly silent; a decorated horse clopped by pulling tourists on a painted cart. My footsteps echoed in the gaps between the churches and the private homes until I rounded a corner into a square. Here, tourists taking photographs of the Carmelite Priory suddenly surrounded me. I walked down another block and it was quiet again. The small town with Arab influences among Catholic churches felt more like a fantasy to me than a reality. I believe this is what makes the atmosphere in Malta so unique.

This fortified city was the capital of Malta until the arrival of the Knights in 1530. Now it has a population of just 300. The name Mdina is from the Arabic word medina. It was a thriving Muslim settlement, and it still has features typical of that period of Arab rule.

When the Order of Saint John took over in Malta, Mdina lost its status as the capital city. During the Great Siege of Malta in 1565, Mdina was the base of the Order's cavalry, carrying out attacks on the invading Ottomans. During the French invasion of Malta, the Maltese rebelled in Mdina and fought the French, succeeding when Malta became part of the British Empire.

Mdina is a main tourist attraction today, hosting 750,000 tourists a year. Cars are not allowed inside and perhaps that is why it earned the name "the Silent City." There was an extensive restoration of the city walls that was completed in 2016.

I visited the Mdina Cathedral, dedicated to St. Paul the Apostle, which was founded in the 12th century. According to tradition, it stands on the site where the Roman governor Publius met St. Paul following his shipwreck on Malta. The church's building and the insides of the church are well worth a visit, so don't skip it when you go to Mdina.

I continued on to visit the old medieval palace Palazzo Falson, the former home of a rich artist and collector named Golcher. It was his home and where he created and displayed his art, and I could see what lay inside a house in the walled town of Mdina. This beautiful palace has elegant rooms filled with art and artifacts, a gorgeous courtyard, and at its center a quiet fountain.

I stopped for lunch at a little restaurant with its own courtyard and got a delicious meal of Burrata with heirloom tomatoes and a fresh piece of fish. After my meal, I continued walking

around this magnificent city, in and out of the maze of alleyways, and streets. At a high point, I looked across the city and could see the whole of Malta. It felt as if I were on a Hollywood movie set from the times of the Knights.

There was one more place I wanted to visit before I headed to the airport for my flight: The Hypogeum of Hal-Saflieni, a subterranean Neolithic structure located in Paola, Malta, 17 minutes away from Mdina. It literally means "underground" in Greek and is believed to have been a sanctuary and ne-cropolis, a large cemetery within a Maltese temple.

It was accidentally discovered in 1902 when workers broke through its roof. The excavations went on for many years, and the discoveries showed that the structure might have been a natural cave. There are burial chambers on upper levels and in the lower chambers. It is believed that the site may have first been used as early as 4000 B.C.

Many objects were recovered from the site, including pot-tery, beads, buttons, and carved figures of humans and animals. A famous discovery was of the Sleeping Lady, be-lieved to represent a mother Goddess. Some of the figures are abstract while others are very realistic, and it is all related to the veneration of the dead and spiritual transformation. It all appealed to the artist in me. The remains of 7,000 indi-viduals were found in the Hypogeum, and most of the skulls were put in the National Museum.

Since on-site scientific research is ongoing, only 80 people can visit per day. Make sure to order your tickets ahead of time and do a little research to prepare for it, so you can really appreciate it all. Note that photography is not allowed, and there are lockers for your possessions. Each tour takes just 10 people on an audio tour, which is very well done, informative and interesting. Even the couple of kids in my group were just as interested in it as the adults. The tour lasted an hour, and I was amazed at how ancient the structure was, as well as by its fantastic condition.

On the ceiling are patterns with different motifs painted with red ocher. One of the central chambers, "The Holy of Holies," appears to be oriented so that light from the winter solstice illuminates its façade from the opening above. Another room called "The Oracle Room" was possibly designed for chanting or drumming, and producing powerful sounds across the Hypogeum.

The visitor center had some more information, but I had to get back to my hotel, pick up my luggage and head to the airport as my time in Malta was coming to an end.

I always feel sad when leaving a destination I enjoyed, but this time I felt a greater melancholy since there was so much more I wanted to see and do here. As we took off, I watched the island receding through the plane's window and thought about my trip and all I wrote about Malta: its beauty, its history, its people, its legends, the food, the sites, and the sea--all these made it a very unique, enchanting, and a special time for me. What an incredible adventure this past week has been. This is truly the ultimate magical island!

The End

Made in the USA
Columbia, SC
19 November 2021